Downhill, Hotdogging, and Cross-Country— If the Snow Isn't Sticky

Words by
Gary Paulsen

Pictures by
Willis Wood
Heinz Kluetmeier

Raintree Publishers
Milwaukee • Toronto • Melbourne • London

Library of Congress Number: 78-26256

  2 3 4 5 6 7 8 9 0 83 82 81 80

Printed and bound in the United States of America.

Library of Congress Cataloging in Publication Data

Paulsen, Gary.
   Downhill, hotdogging and cross-country — if the
snow isn't sticky.

   SUMMARY: A humorous commentary on different aspects
of skiing using photographs of professional skiers.
   1. Skis and skiing — Anecdotes, facetiae, satire,
etc. — Juvenile literature. [1. Skis and skiing]
I. Wood, Willis. II. Kluetmeier, Heinz. III. Title.
GV854.3.P38   796.9'3'0207   78-26256
ISBN 0-8172-0187-4 lib. bdg.

SKIING

Skiing is a fairly simple sport. You just put a couple of sticks on your feet, ride a chair to the top of a mountain, and then slide down. Fast. If you're an expert you might come down very fast. If you're not an expert you might come down end over end.

You still get down the mountain.

DOWNHILL

There are many ways to get down the mountain. You can go through the trees, for instance. This is very popular with new skiers who haven't learned to turn just yet.

WITHDRAWN

You can also go down on your back.
This looks a little strange but saves a lot
of wear and tear on your skis.

No matter how you go down, be sure to wear mirrored goggles. That way nobody can tell when your eyes are closed. Which is most of the time.

Looking cool is a big part of skiing. This includes making smooth turns, wearing space-age boots, and having hair all over your face. Be sure the boots are orange. They might be the only thing showing, and it makes them easy to see.

If you should start going fast — very fast — try not to scream. It scares the other skiers. Just keep a smile until you wipe out at the bottom of the mountain.

RACING

Racing is a whole separate part of skiing. The idea is to get your sticks to the bottom of the mountain before the other person. Naturally. That's what racing is, right? But then they throw in some vertical poles and jumps and trees and rocks and. . .

Sometimes it's everything you can do just to get through without breaking something.

A good start is important when racing. Sit back and study the hill carefully. You might not want to go.

If you go, push off hard! Don't change your mind halfway through the start. That's how to get a mountain named after you.

The main thing to remember about skiing downhill in a race is to stay calm. Keep your tongue in your mouth. Otherwise it will get cold. Don't open your eyes until you get to the bottom. If you do, it will just scare you.

For jumps while racing, the best method is the squat-scream. Just drop down and yell until you hit the ground. The leaning-scream works well for taking down vertical poles sideways during the slalom.

Fancy goggles can make almost anything work. But not going off the side of a jump. Nothing can make that work.

Sometimes a good grimace will help get
you through the slalom gates. But
don't hold it too long. It might get frozen
on. And how would a grimace of fear
look to the news cameras if you win?

HOT-DOGGING

Hotdogging is supposed to be free-form skiing. Do anything you want — go crazy. Actually, some of the best hotdoggers are beginners that get pushed down expert slopes when they aren't looking. Haven't you ever wondered why they never show them landing?

CROSS-COUNTRY

The hardest thing about cross-country skiing is memory. You go out there and hack around all day, having a great time. But you've got to remember to come back. And it's always twice as far home as it was going out. . .

Of course, if you have somebody carry you, it makes it easier. Or if you go in crowds. Just don't fall down in front of the pack.

The best part of cross-country, and all other skiing, is that it's truly a great way to get outdoors. To see nature. As long as you like the color blue.

Blue noses. Blue ears. Blue cheeks. . .